Meet Robyn Greene

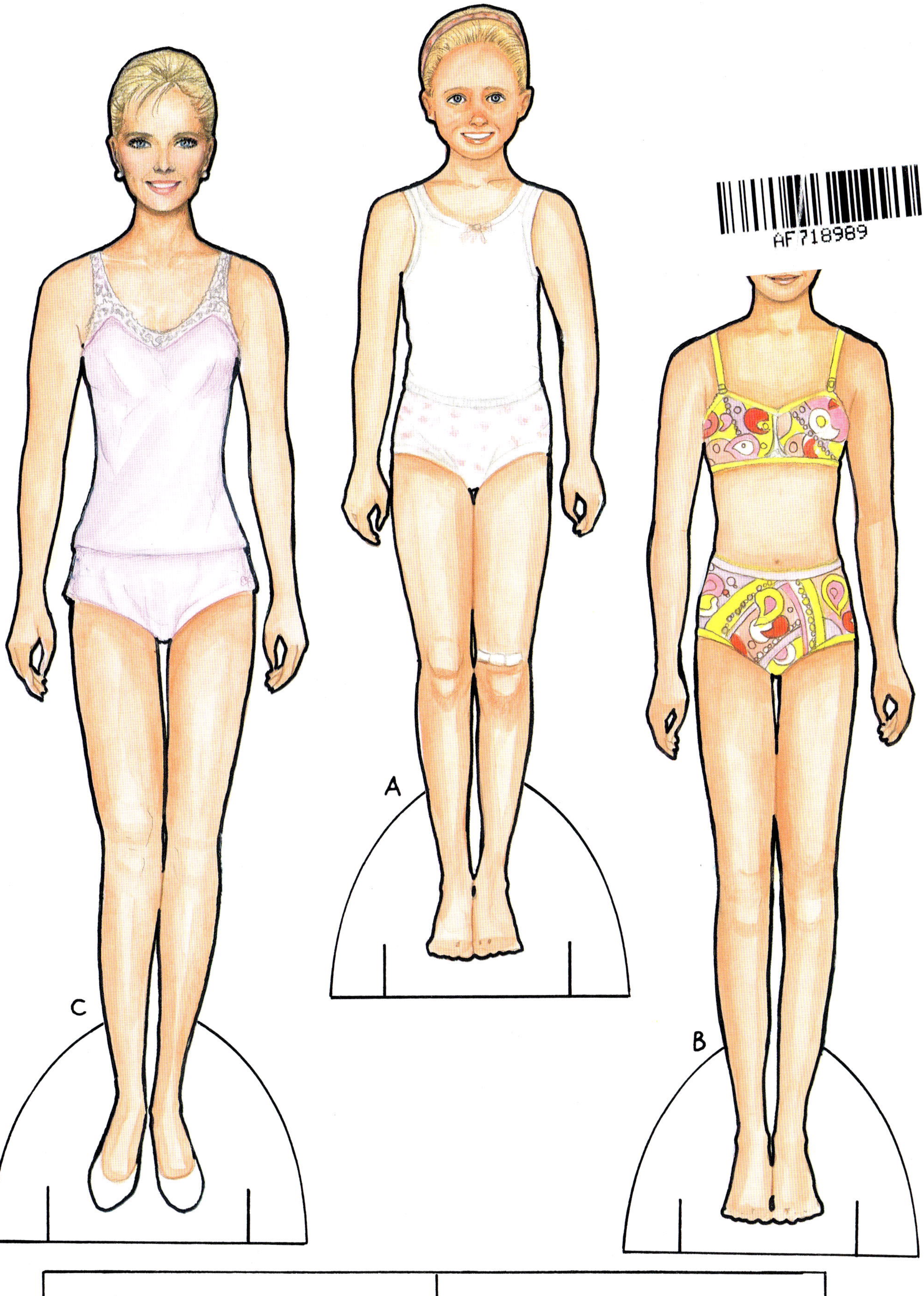

This is her best friend Judi

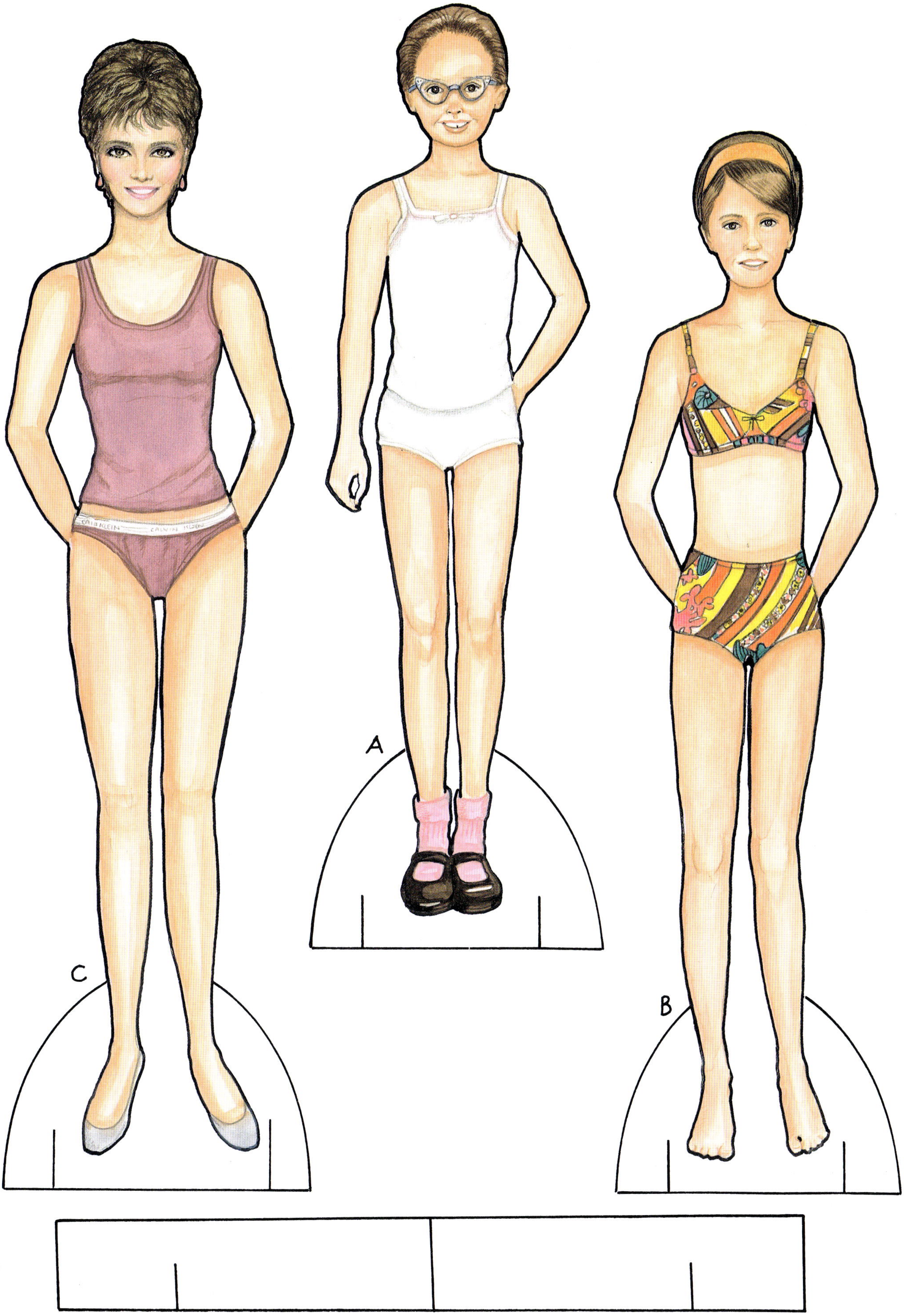

This Year's Girl

This Year's Girl

by Sally Edelstein

1985

A Dolphin Book
Doubleday & Company, Inc.
Garden City, New York

ISBN 0-385-19828-0

Typography by David November
Printed in Japan
9 8 7 6 5 4 3 2

Once upon a time, but not too long ago, when mothers kaffeeklatsched with the girls and fathers knew best, when we liked Ike and loved Lucy, and Sunday nights meant Ed Sullivan, there existed many new magic kingdoms.

And in these kingdoms of vast shopping centers and bowling lanes lived thousands of young couples, babies in tow, babies on the way. Where once there were many vacant lots and potato fields, there now bloomed a dozen Sunnyvales, a score of Pleasant Valleys, and a gross of Maplewoods.

And in these magic kingdoms the family reigned supreme. Fresh from the victory of battles fought on foreign shores, the young men rescued their damsels who had been waiting for them at home, married them, and whisked them off to their magic kingdom, where they proceeded to produce a multitude of princes and princesses. And in this kingdom nothing would be more valued than they.

And the kingdom grew...Housing developments sprouted, new schools were built to educate the princes and princesses, new shopping centers catered to their every whim and taste.

The young couples in the kingdom needed some guidance in raising their princely progeny. Many sought the kingdom's oracle: a wise man, Benjamin Spock. And thus spoke the oracle: Indulge! Pamper! Permit! But even the great oracle could not provide all the wisdom. For there was one far greater and more powerful than he: a revered member in each household who carried great influence, who kept the princes and princesses amused, and who would always be there for them. And this revered member was called Philco, Admiral, or Emerson.

And from Philco the princes and princesses learned the most important lessons of their lives right from the start — the value of the new and improved. What is good today can only be improved tomorrow with something better. They would learn to become the

consummate consumers. The lessons of Philco would last for a thousand tomorrows.

And it was this magic kingdom, this promised land, that lured Gerald and Helen Greene and their six-month-old daughter Robin from their comfortable, familiar, albeit small garden apartment in Forest Hills, Queens, to the fabled south shore of Long Island. Like their immigrant parents before them who crossed the ocean to Ellis Island in search of a better life, these potato field pioneers sought out the better life the suburbs had to offer. (A growing child needs fresh air!)

It was a dream they often fantasized about in their letters to one another while Jerry was stationed in the Philippines during the war. The scenario always played the same — his safe return, the wedding, the house in the country with a yard big enough for all their babies to play in.

And so indeed they were married in

the fall of 1950, and returning from a honeymoon in the Catskills they lived briefly with Helen's parents on a shady street in Flatbush. Not a particularly ideal situation for newlyweds, but what with the housing shortage, it suited them fine.

Jerry's paycheck — that of a junior account executive with a Madison Avenue advertising agency — was meager, but they managed to save enough to move into their own, small garden apartment in Queens. Although nearly twenty-four years old, Helen was the kind of girl who had never ventured far from home; and so, although the move was right across the bridge, Helen got into the habit of calling her mother at least once a day (thus playing the role of dutiful daughter, just as her mother had with her own mother).

Life was pleasant enough. Jerry worked close enough to home — only a few stops on the F train. Helen spent her days tidying up the three-room apartment, grateful for the new Electrolux Jerry had given her for her

birthday (What a doll!). Housework came to a halt at 12:30 P.M. so Helen could watch "Search for Tomorrow." For diversion, she skimmed the latest Book-of-the-Month-Club selection (after all, she did major in English literature at NYU).

Evenings were spent watching television on their new fifteen-inch Philco (Jerry particularly chuckled over Sid Caesar and Bilko). Once a week they bowled in a league, twice winning trophies! While Jerry attended night classes two evenings a week, Helen played bridge with the girls.

Occasionally Helen would get playful and experiment with some exotic dish featured in the *Ladies' Home Journal* to add a festive touch to their fairly regular lives. Or she might rearrange the blonde wood living room furniture set and dare Jerry to notice just to keep him on his toes. (She tried dying her hair blonde once just to see if blondes had more fun... They didn't.)

It seemed as though they had just set up house when in May of 1952 their lit-

tle girl, Robin Beth, was born. Learning that this was to be Helen's only child made the joyful event all the more special.

Now that they were an official family, they spent several Sundays driving their 1949 De Soto over the highways of Long Island in search of their dream house.

After several months they found just the right community to raise little Robin in — good schools, plenty of shopping, and a sewer system installed and paid for!

And in the very house next-door was another little girl just Robin's age, named Judy, that she could play with when she got older.

And so on that same cold day in November when General Eisenhower became the President-elect, Helen packed the last of her Harlequinware dishes into their boxes, and with great expectations the Greenes moved into their own split-level dream house in the heart of suburbia...

This Year's Girl

Robin was her mother's perfect little girl— ballet lessons

Robin was her father's little princess—Birthday Party

When We Grow Up – Robin

When We Grow Up – Judy

Aa Bb Cc Dd Ee Ff
School
Kellogg's SUGAR FROSTED FLAKES
INSTANT Tang
starting the day off right
Breck clean hair
THE NEW BASIC READER
Robin B Green
We Read Pictures
SCHOOL
ROCKY pencil holder
pencil case to hold plenty of sharpened #2 pencils
64 Crayola CRAYONS
BUILT IN SHARPENER
Pony Tail
change purse for milk money
GUMBY
MILK
WONDER
ENRICHED BREAD
show 'n tell
MR MACHINE
Robin trades her peanut butter and jelly sandwich for a bologna sandwich plus a Twinkie!
...and his name is Mr. Machine
OBEY TRAFFIC SIGNALS
HEADING
GREETING
MESSAGE
CLOSING
SIGNATURE
WHERE DO YOU LIVE?
HUT
IGLOO
RANCH HOUSE
BOOK WEEK
HAWAII
OUR 50TH STATE

Days
Gg Hh Ii Jj Kk L
Calling All GIRLS
THE FIVE CHINESE BROTHERS
HOP ON POP
By Dr. Seuss
Book club selections
Smoking ...its up to you
Robin learns to stay out of smoke-filled high school girls' room
Great American Negroes
The JETSONS
Robin would rather read The Jetsons than watch the space shot
caught chewing gum!
My Weekly Reader
JOHN FITZGERALD KENNEDY
OUR NEW PRESIDENT
JAN. 1961
STUDENTS FOR KENNEDY
NIXON
EXPERIENCE COUNTS
Mom has milk and cookies waiting after school
Nestles Quik
Robin roots for JFK – he's cuter than Nixon!
GRADE 4 CHRISTMAS PAGEANT
FIRE PREVENTION WEEK
Drink MILK
FEBRUARY
12
22

Esso
How I spent my summer ~~vacashun~~ vacation
Sept. 7
Are we there yet?
Stuckey's
PECAN SHOPPE
neat magnetic dogs, bought at rest stop
Holiday Inn
THE WORLD'S INNKEEPER
MIAMI
Miami troll
CAPE CANAVERA
gen-u-ine stuffed miniature crocodile
Robin likes their restrooms best
Sinclair
space ships - just like on TV

Bestest friends – when boys still had cooties

They had one word for boys:
Y-U-C-K

Hello Barbie
Barbie
Ken®
Midge®
Allan®
Barbie learns early and snags a doctor
modestly attired but oh-so-appealing
just right for sippin' sodas with Ken
Dream House® for Barbie and Ken
Barbie Dream House
Barbie Sings
(once legally married)
Barbie – 11 inches of sure sex appeal
Ken – every inch a real man
M
BABY SIT

Class Report – Fallout Shelter Survival Kit

The year mothers were invited to school – "A Special Film for Girls"

Nov. 22, 1963 – the year the father-daughter dinner was cancelled

Girl Talk – Slumber Party

Sleep-Away Camp

Developing Tastes

Holy Twinkies – Thin is In

First Romance – "I Wanna Be Bobby's Girl"

California Dreamin'

POP
POW
WHAM
Brillo soap pads
Brillo
Campbell's
SOUP
7up
OH, MIDGE. WHY MUST THEY ALWAYS HURT ME? (SOB) WHY ME?
BATMAN
POP
Holy Shopping Mall! Robin Goes Pop!

Secret Dreams – Modeling Mania

And the Beat Goes On...

Basement Shindig – Making Out – a – go – go

High School: Scheduled

Days — Scheduled Nights

Jr. Prom – Waiting Up

Summer Before Graduation – Cruisin' and Boozin'

Graduation – Do Your Own Thing

Hopes for the future –
All you need is LUV
DO YOU REALLY LOVE ME?
Rod McKuen
LOVE STORY
by ERICH SEGAL
NEW!
duet
CRACKER
The Newlywed Game
SURREALISTIC PILLOW
JEFFERSON AIRPLANE
Love American Style
The way to become The Sensuous Woman by "J"
LOVE'S FRESH LEMON CLEANSE
EAU DE LOVE SPRAY
Everything you always wanted to know about sex*
Explained by David Reuben, M.D.
*BUT WERE AFRAID TO ASK
Robin wants to be IN Love
Judy wants to be in a Love-IN
I Love You This Much
BE MINE
Togetherness-We Can Make It
BE MINE

change to doll C

College Life – What a Drag

Liberate!

liberated hair – look like a prostitute in Klute
Fuck housework
Robin lowers her hemline as her consciousness is raised
Robin liberates her name to Robyn
Ms.
OUR BODIES OURSELVES
A BOOK BY AND FOR WOMEN
WOMEN UNITE
liberated bodies
new freedom
FLUSHABLE
Kotex
FDS
The Female Eunuch
liberated cigarettes
eve
liberated TV. It's OK to be 30 and single
TV GUIDE
VE YOU HAD
E PILL TODAY
liberated hair – permed in sympathy with oppressed black sisters
liberated hot pants – take that, you male chauvinist pigs!
Judy liberates her name to Judi
freedom now
freedom now
freedom now

Tuning Into Nature

Robyn meets Jeffrey and the Karma is right

Postgraduate Wars— Living in the Here and Now
GROWTH GAMES
How to Tune In Yourself, Your Family, Your Friends
Communicate! Relate!
I AM SO GLAD that you are here
it helps me to realize how beautiful my world is
BURRY
HappYolks
Have a nice day!
I'M OK— YOU'RE OK
A PRACTICAL GUIDE TO TRANSACTIONAL ANALYSIS
Robyn relates to plants at the LIBERATED FICUS PLANT SHOP 3 times a week
Jeff relates at the Human Relations Center part-time
Judi has a touching group experience at Esalen
Jonathan Livingston Seagull
You have the freedom to be yourself.... here and now.

Checking Out Reality – Inflation and the Energy Crisis

Robyn learns to be assertive, Jeff to be sensitive

New Roles

Giving Each Other More Space — Trying the Singles Scene
what's your sign?
Charlie
MARY QUANT CRAYONS
MARY QUANT CRAYONS
COSMOPOLITAN
"Can Robyn be that Cosmo Girl?
Linda Goodman
SUN SIGNS
How to Really Know Your
RG
getting into backgammon
New School Bulletin Fall 1975
alternative singles scene
phone-mate
no messages —what a downer
MUSK SHAVE CREAM
Jeff bares it all!
CONAIR PRO-STYLE
Power Hold
MACHO
cologne
Le Brief
French bikinis for men
Binaca
the Binaca blast
FOXY
Let's Boogie
PINBALL WIZARD

Finalizing the Parameters of their Interface

Coping with Depression – Different Strokes for Different Folks
Robyn joins the ME Generation
HALSTON
Calvin Klein
People
WOODY ALLEN
the panacea of the '70s
CONTROLLED
For R GREEN
ONE TABLET
VALIUM
run your problems away
gossip
bloomingdale's
Perrier
Judi
Judi copes in a hot tub
Runner's Day-by-Day Log
SELF
Famous Amos
learning how to be your own best friend
designer binges
watch someone more neurotic than yourself
PET ROCK
Robyn's mood ring turns black
to fend off loneliness
MAY THE FORCE BE WITH YOU
ROCHE 5 VALIUM
MAY THE FORCE BE WITH YOU

Laid Back in California – Visiting Judi

Dance Fever

DONNA SUMMER
cruisin'
ODYSSEY
BOLT.
GQ
THAT NEW YORK DAZZLE
PLAYBILL
A CHORUS LINE
A CHORUS LINE
A CHORUS LINE
ALVIN AILEY
AMERICAN DANCE THEATRE
PLAYBILL
Dancin!

Robyn and Jeff get on the fast track
to go
Robyn listens to stress reduction
tapes on her walk-man
SONY
WALKMAN
SYLVIA PORTER'S NEW MONEY BOOK FOR THE 80'S
THE WOMAN'S DRESS FOR SUCCESS BOOK
Esquire
Who Will Make Money in the '80s?
go for it
We need Reagan
"No nonsense panty hose"
PBS
Robyn's King Tut mug
JERRY RUBIN BUSINESS NETWORKING SALON CARD
PERMANENT CARD
EVERY WEDNESDAY AT STUDIO 54
Robyn carries sensible pumps for the office
networking — DO IT!
DANNON Plain LOWFAT YOGURT
TaB
no one penciled in for lunch — eat at desk

High School Reunion – Different Wavelengths, Common Concerns

Will Robyn lose Jeff to the World of Video?

Robyn Wants to Be a Princess – Summer in the Hamptons

Turning 30 – Recalling Childhood Expectations (Unmet)

10 Years of Interfacing — Metamorphoses

Mr. and Mrs. Gerald Greene
request the honour of your company
at the wedding of their daughter
Robyn Beth Greene
a reception fit for a princess
wedding announcement
PETER BROWN
make-up
The Plaza
Taittinger
HAWAII
Hawaiian honeymoon
Our Wedding
VHS
VIDEOS by Doug Campbell

Judi works it out, Robyn works it off

Robyn and Jeff go for it – "We get pregnant"

This Year's Girl

ACKNOWLEDGMENTS

Once upon a time, on a faraway island called Manhattan, lived a lovely princess named Sally. And this princess, like so many other princesses, lived in a tiny studio in a fine co-op castle.

But this princess had a peculiar habit of saving everything she ever owned. The room spilled over with Barbie dolls and smile buttons, Archie comics and Beatle dolls, love beads and quiche pans, so that soon there was no room left for the princess to move.

All the other princes and princesses loved to visit the princess because of all the wonderful treasures. They too had once owned the same valuables, but theirs were long since gone. What wonderful stories these treasures told, what warm memories they evoked.

As she sat amongst all the clutter, the princess often thought, "If only I could create a book and put all my treasures in it so that all the other princes and princesses could enjoy them for ever!" And the treasures could tell the story of herself and of all the other princes and princesses she knew.

But the princess was unsure of how to perform this mighty task, so she turned to those more knowing for advice.

First she turned to her wise old friend Jerry Martin, the kingdom's sage, for counsel. He gave her confidence, for he had faith in her even when the princess didn't and made her believe in herself. "No sage could be more insightful," thought the princess.

Next, she sought the help of the kingdom's wizard, Doug Campbell, who performed miracles too numerous to name. For the wizard had a heart of gold and could magically transform himself into whatever it was the princess needed. "No wizard could be more patient and kind," thought the princess.

Of course the princess' parents, Queen Betty and King Marvin, were eager to help their princess in whatever way they could. "No parents could be more loving and supportive and generous than mine," thought the grateful princess.

And certainly none could be more trusted and valued than the princess' brother Andrew. For Andrew was the kingdom's scribe, and his mind was filled with vast volumes of knowledge and information. "No brother could be more helpful and knowledgeable than mine," thought the princess. The princess felt lucky to have such good and devoted friends and family.

So she wrote and researched. She painted and drew. She had no time left for parties and fun. But her hard work paid off. One day the princess showed her efforts to a visiting thespian named Gordon, who laughed and chuckled and saw himself in the book and knew that other princes and princesses would feel the same way. So he sent her off with an invitation to the Castle of Dreams Come True — the palace of Doubleday.

Before she knew it a young, princely editor named Adrian Zackheim stood before her. It was her fairy godfather editor. "Hurry, child," he said. "You are going to do the book." The princess could hardly believe her ears! And with a wave of his magic wand he made a contract appear. With the help of the princess' attorney, Hershel Katz, the contract was signed.

So the princess scurried back home to work and hermetically sealed herself off in her ivory tower studio for months at a time. She received few visitors and was glad for the company her Sony Trinitron gave her. The princess worked into the wee hours of the morning and was grateful to the kingdom's jesters — Johnny Carson, David Letterman, and Mary Tyler Moore (in reruns) for keeping her entertained throughout the late nights.

Soon, though, the princess summoned the help of two little elves — Robin Barnes and Miriam Campiz — who, equipped with T-squares and paintbrushes, worked hard and long into the night to help the princess finish the book. The elves rarely complained and were as dedicated as two elves could be. "How lucky I am to have such skilled elves," the princess thought.

But soon her days became topsy-turvy. Days turned into nights and summer spilled into fall, and the princess began to feel the weight of the project and soon grew weary. The princess worried, wondering if indeed she could finish the book.

Now a handsome prince named Peter Brown, who lived in the same co-op castle, heard of the lovely princess and her plight and rode up to see her. Instantly he knew just how to help her, and with his fine artistic skills and clever ways he saved the princess from panic. "How fortunate I am to have such a talented and loving friend," thought the princess. "Oh, how can I ever thank you," she cried. For indeed the book was saved.

With renewed strength, the princess completed the work — and so she waved good-bye to the elves and to the handsome prince and rode off to the Castle of Dreams Come True.

At the palace all the workers scurried about to turn the work into a book. The princess could hardly believe her eyes! With a touch of her magic wand, the palace art director, Diana Klemin, turned the stack of paintings and hundreds of words into a real-life book. And the court calligrapher, Paul Shaw, was called in to transform all the words into type so that all the princes and princesses of the kingdom could read and enjoy.

So the princess went home to her tiny studio in the co-op castle, satisfied in the knowledge that all her treasures were safe inside a book and that soon all would know the story about the princes and princesses of the land and their cherished treasures.

WE GRATEFULLY ACKNOWLEDGE THE FOLLOWING:

Wham-O® is a registered trademark of Kransco Manufacturing, Inc.

Speedy Alka Seltzer Copyright © Miles Laboratories, Inc., 1952

BARBIE, KEN, MIDGE, ALLAN and DREAM HOUSE are trademarks of Mattel, Inc. used with permission © Mattel, Inc. 1985.

Rocky and Boris Badinoff characters © 1985 P.A.T.-Ward

Buster Brown used with permission of Brown Shoe Co., a member of the Brown Group

Madeline illustration from MADELINE by Ludwig Bemelmans © 1939 by Ludwig Bemelmans, copyright renewed 1967 by Mrs. Madeleine Bemelmans and Mrs. Barbara Bemelmans Marciano, reprinted by permission of Viking Penguin Inc.

*Indicates Trademark of Warner Bros. Inc. © 1985.

Mighty Mouse character reproduced by permission of Viacom International Inc.

Cheerios® is a registered trademark of General Mills, Inc. and is being used with permission of General Mills, Inc.

†*Tony the Tiger* and *Crackle!* and character designs are trademarks of Kellogg Company, © 1985 Kellogg, all rights reserved. Used by permission.

Tootle the Train, Scuffy the Tugboat, The Taxi That Hurried, Sleeping Bear, Tubby and Little Lulu © Western Publishing Company, Inc. Reprinted by permission.

Richie Rich © Harvey Features

Casper © Harvey Cartoons

Hot Stuff © Harvey Features

Little Lotta © Harvey Features

WOODY WOODPECKER® © 1957 Walter Lantz Productions, Inc. All rights reserved.

Illustration of "Babar" from BABAR LOSES HIS CROWN, by Laurent De Brunhoff. Copyright © 1967 by Random House, Inc. Reprinted by permission of Random House, Inc.

These are her parents –

And these are the men in her life –

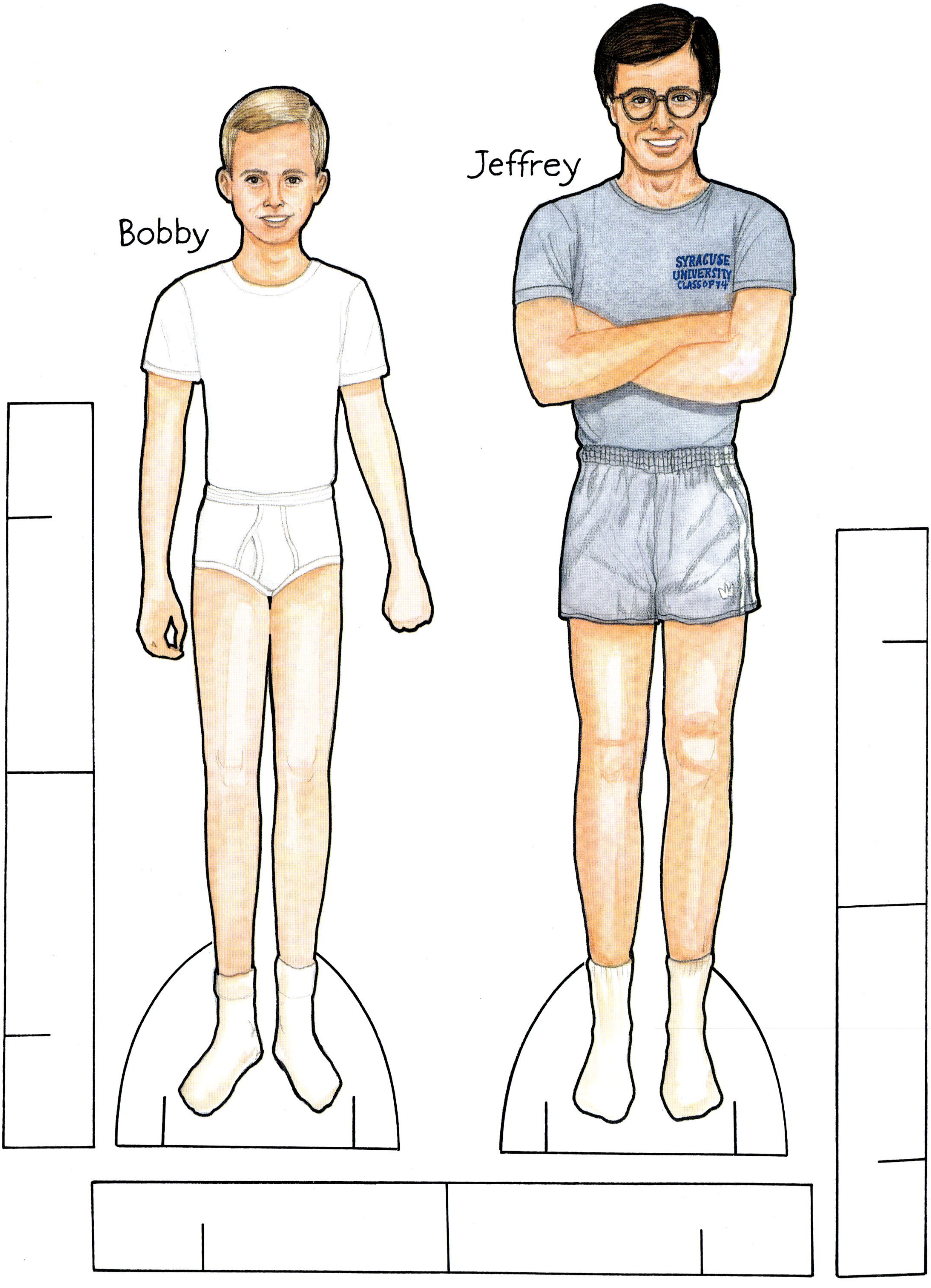